HUMAN-MADE DISASTERS

OIL SPILLS

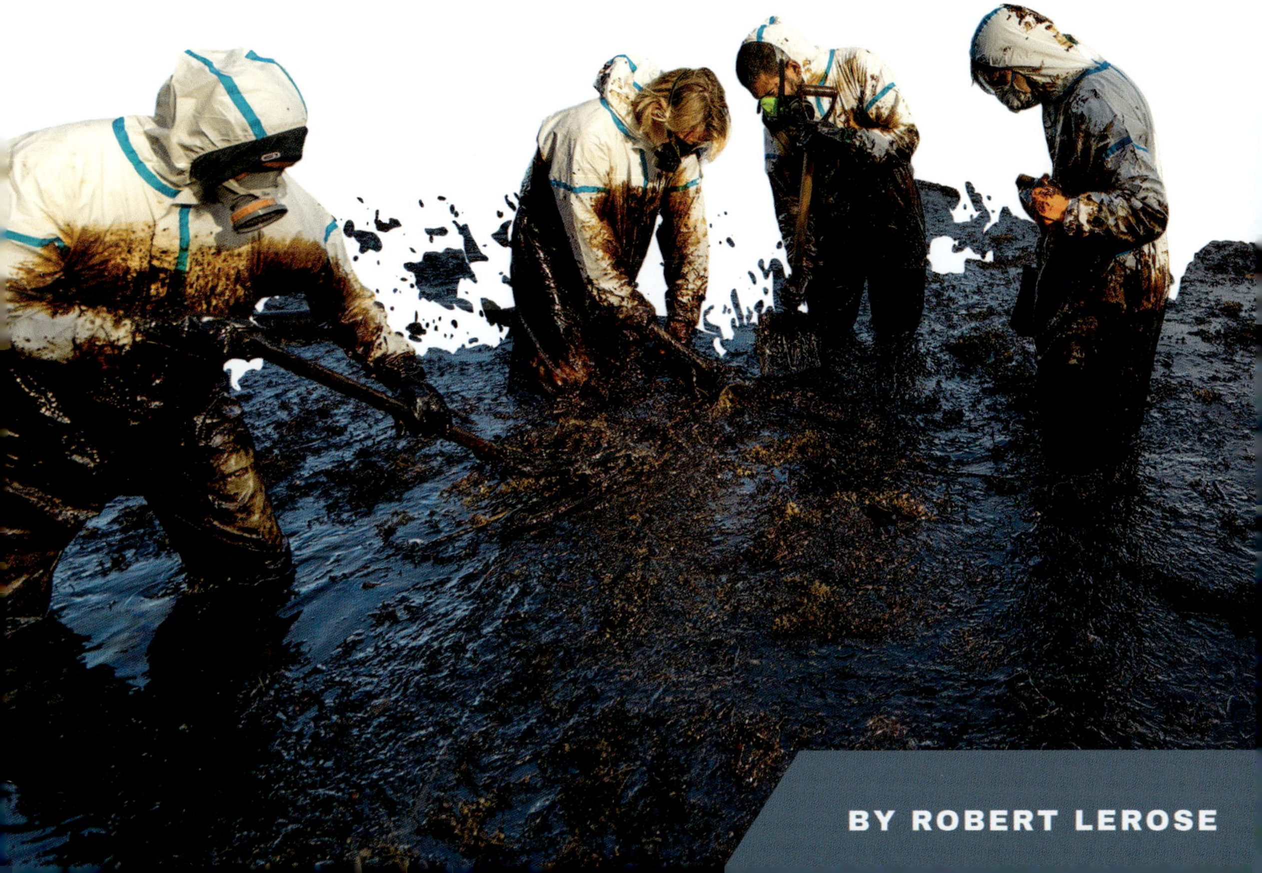

BY ROBERT LEROSE

WWW.APEXEDITIONS.COM

Apex is distributed by North Star Editions:
sales@northstareditions.com | 888-417-0195

Produced for Apex by Red Line Editorial.

Photographs ©: Shutterstock Images, cover, 1, 9, 10–11, 12, 13, 14–15, 26–27, 29; Charlie Riedel/AP Images, 4–5; Gerald Herbert/AP Images, 6–7; US Coast Guard, 8; NOAA/AP Images, 16–17; John Gaps III/AP Images, 18–19, 20; Bob Jordan/AP Images, 21; Jae C. Hong/AP Images, 22–23; Gwendoline Defente/Etat Major des Armees/AP Images, 24–25

Library of Congress Control Number: 2023921994

ISBN
978-1-63738-928-7 (hardcover)
978-1-63738-968-3 (paperback)
979-8-89250-063-0 (ebook pdf)
979-8-89250-026-5 (hosted ebook)

Printed in the United States of America
Mankato, MN
082024

NOTE TO PARENTS AND EDUCATORS

Apex books are designed to build literacy skills in striving readers. Exciting, high-interest content attracts and holds readers' attention. The text is carefully leveled to allow students to achieve success quickly. Additional features, such as bolded glossary words for difficult terms, help build comprehension.

TABLE OF CONTENTS

CHAPTER 1

A HUGE LEAK

It is April 20, 2010. Workers are busy on the Deepwater Horizon **rig**. They drill down to reach oil under the ocean.

Deepwater Horizon was located in the Gulf of Mexico.

Suddenly, an explosion rocks the rig. Gas rushes upward and catches fire. Workers jump into the ocean to escape. Oil gushes from the hole they drilled.

The explosion killed 11 workers and hurt 17 others.

FAST FACT

The leak lasted 87 days. About 206 million gallons (780 million L) of oil poured out.

Two days later, the rig crumbles into the ocean. Meanwhile, oil continues to pour into the water.

The US Coast Guard sent ships to save the burning oil rig. But the rig sank.

Many animals got covered in oil after the Deepwater Horizon spill. Hundreds of thousands died.

SPILL DAMAGE

The oil spill covered more than 57,500 square miles (149,900 sq km). The oil floated on top of the water. It **polluted** beaches.

CHAPTER 2

HOW SPILLS HAPPEN

Some oil spills take place when crews are drilling. **Equipment** can break. Or people can make mistakes.

In the early 2020s, people drilled more than 50,000 oil wells each year.

Tankers can carry up to four million barrels of oil. One barrel holds 42 gallons (159 L) of oil.

Oil can also leak while being **transported**. Big storms at sea can overturn ships. Pipelines can spring leaks.

FAST FACT

Strong winds can damage oil rigs. They can break pipes or cause rigs to lose power.

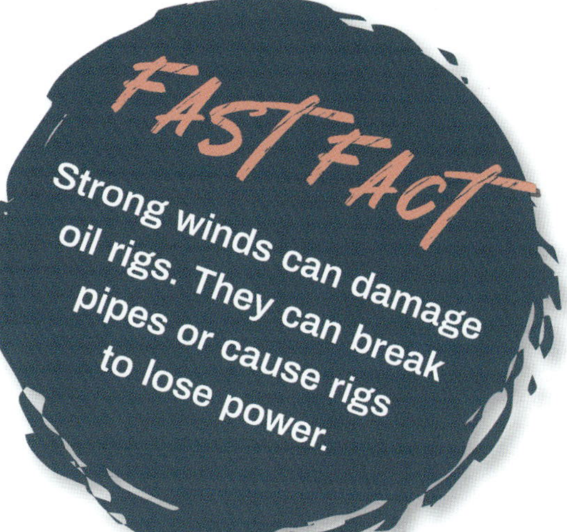

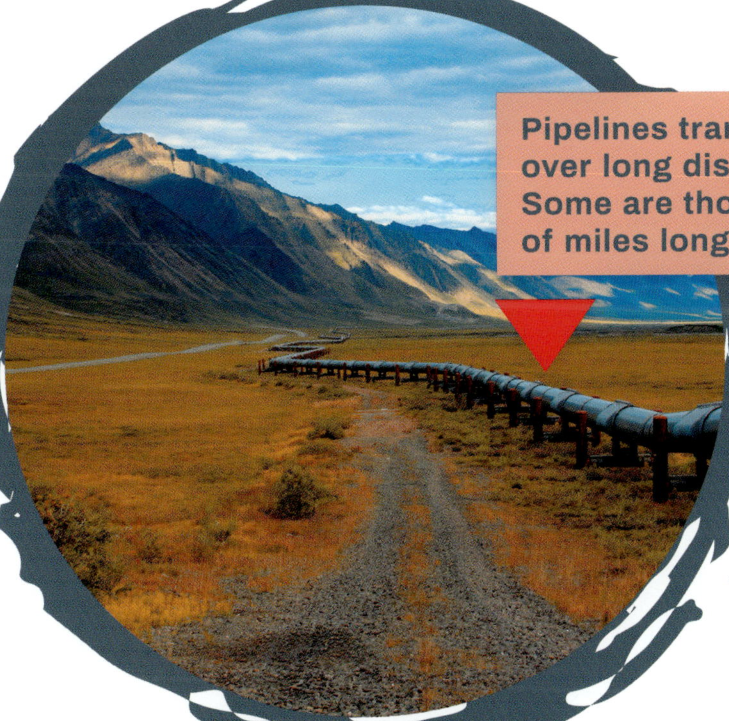

Pipelines transport oil over long distances. Some are thousands of miles long.

An oil spill can spread far and fast. Often, oil floats in a thin layer on top of the water. It can harm animals and their **habitats**.

LOTS OF PROBLEMS

Oil can coat animals' fur or feathers. That makes it hard for them to stay warm and dry. Animals get sick if they try to lick the oil off. Eating food covered in oil can poison animals, too.

People work to clean animals that have been covered in oil.

CHAPTER 3

OIL SPILLS EVERYWHERE

In 1979, a rig exploded in the Gulf of Mexico. More than 126 million gallons (477 million L) of oil leaked out. It stained many beaches black.

The Ixtoc 1 rig leaked oil into the Gulf of Mexico for nine months.

On March 24, 1989, a ship was bringing oil from Alaska. The ship hit a **reef**. About 11 million gallons (42 million L) of oil spilled into the water.

LAND LEAK

The biggest land accident took place in 1992. A well in Uzbekistan exploded. It released oil for two months. About 88 million gallons (333 million L) of oil escaped.

The *Exxon Valdez* spill in 1989 killed more than 200,000 animals. They included birds, seals, and whales.

During the Persian Gulf War (1990–1991), oil fields in Kuwait burned for months.

In 1991, Iraq was at war with Kuwait. Iraq's army set fire to Kuwait's oil fields. Iraqi soldiers also dumped huge amounts of oil into the Persian Gulf.

FAST FACT

The Persian Gulf oil spill was the largest in history.

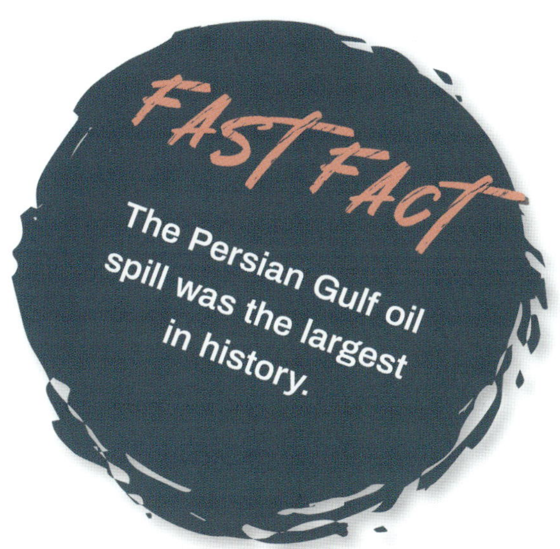

Hundreds of millions of gallons of oil spilled into the Persian Gulf. Oil washed up on beaches.

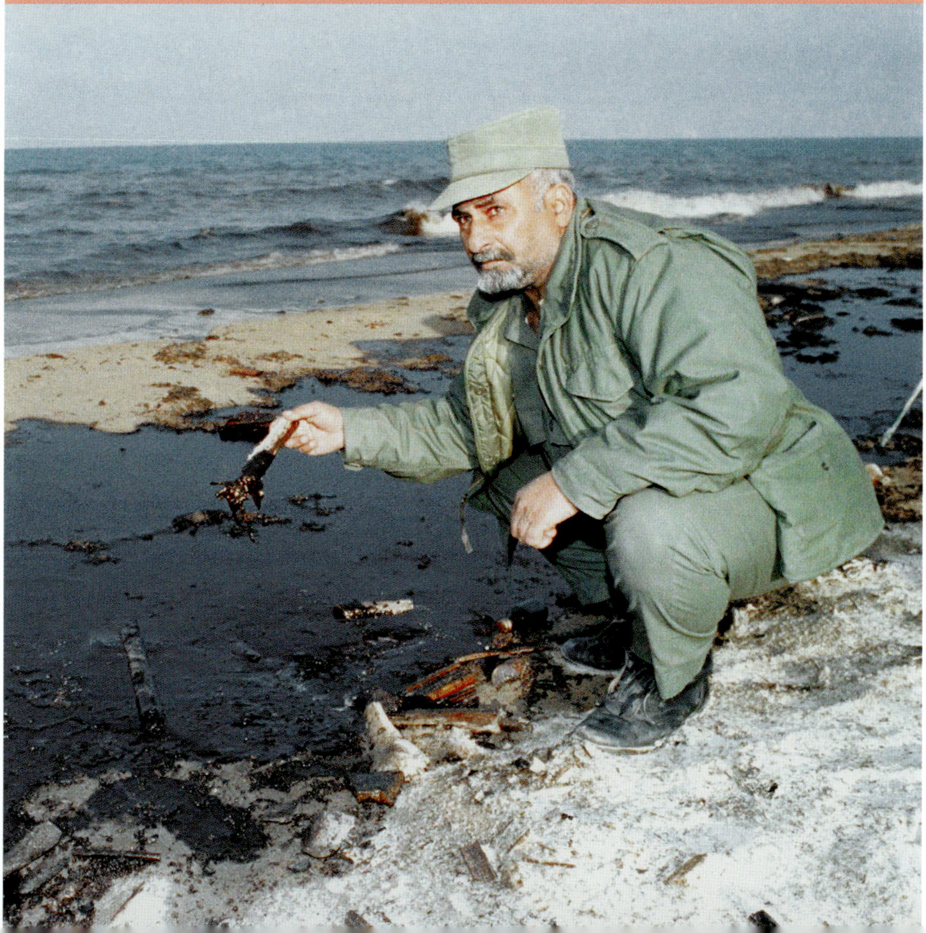

CHAPTER 4

CLEANING UP

After oil spills, people may place booms in the water. These floating barriers stop oil from spreading. People also use skimmers. These tools scoop oil from the surface.

Some booms go around ships to trap oil. Other booms are placed near land to keep oil away.

However, oil is very difficult to remove. It spreads quickly. But booms and skimmers tend to be slow.

FAST FACT

One quart (0.9 L) of oil can create an oil **slick** the size of three football fields.

Large spills can cost billions of dollars to clean up.

As a result, people work hard to prevent spills. They inspect ships and pipelines. They look for problems. They also train cleanup crews to work quickly and safely.

EYES IN THE SKY

Satellites help people watch for oil spills. They can track where the oil moves. That helps **notify** cleanup crews. A quick response can lessen the damage.

Cleanup teams may use shovels to remove oil from shorelines.

COMPREHENSION QUESTIONS

Write your answers on a separate piece of paper.

1. Write a few sentences describing the main ideas of Chapter 4.

2. Do you think people are doing enough to prevent oil spills? Why or why not?

3. How long did the Deepwater Horizon rig leak oil?

   A. 20 days
   B. 87 days
   C. 140 days

4. Why would a faster cleanup response be helpful?

   A. Cleanup crews could stop oil before it spreads.
   B. Cleanup crews would have more time to rest.
   C. Cleanup crews could learn more about pollution.

5. What does **barriers** mean in this book?

After oil spills, people may place booms in the water. These floating ***barriers*** *stop oil from spreading.*

- **A.** things that pour water
- **B.** things that block the way
- **C.** things that light up

6. What does **inspect** mean in this book?

They ***inspect*** *ships and pipelines. They look for problems.*

- **A.** check something carefully
- **B.** take something apart
- **C.** forget about something

Answer key on page 32.

GLOSSARY

equipment

Tools or machines used to do a job.

habitats

The places where animals normally live.

notify

To tell someone about something.

polluted

Made dirty or unsafe.

reef

A chain of rocks, sand, or coral near the surface of water.

rig

A structure used to drill for oil.

satellites

Spacecraft that orbit Earth, often to collect information.

slick

A layer of oil that floats over an area of water.

transported

Moved from one place to another.

BOOKS

Buckley, James, Jr. *Deepwater Disaster: Seabird Rescue!* Minneapolis: Bearport Publishing, 2021.

Cella, Clara. *Underwater Construction Workers.* Minneapolis: Lerner Publications, 2023.

Rebman, Nick. *Earth-Friendly Energy.* Mendota Heights, MN: Focus Readers, 2022.

ONLINE RESOURCES

Visit **www.apexeditions.com** to find links and resources related to this title.

ABOUT THE AUTHOR

Robert Lerose has a giant tree in his backyard that he says hello to every morning. Robert likes to write about the natural world and protecting the planet. He hates oil spills.

INDEX

ANSWER KEY:
1. Answers will vary; 2. Answers will vary; 3. B; 4. A; 5. B; 6. A